THE NAVIGATOR WITHIN

LIFE-CHANGING FORMULAS FROM THE HEART OF MT. SHASTA

Allou Guthmiller

The Navigator Within

TXu 1-790-812

ISBN 978-0-9850236-1-4
Library of Congress Control Number: 2012907535
Phone 808-366-4389
www.ClaimYourPowerToHeal.com
Cover Art: Shern Sharma
Page Layout and Formatting: Silverlining Designs

Acknowledgements

The inspiration behind these "formulas for change" came from my daily experience of living in the sacred foothills below Mount Shasta.

With gratitude for my own transformation, I thank the Divine Presence that guides me daily and has the power to transform us all.

I am deeply thankful for the gift of these formulas, as they continue to mold my own life daily.

I am privileged to express my deepest appreciation for my patient and creative son. His clarity and brainstorming with me added to the finishing touches of this book.

Finally, I thank you, the reader. May your life be enriched and blessed.

Introduction

This book was written during an extraordinary time, a time when old systems of being were on the verge of collapse, when the world recognized the unsustainable course it had set for itself and decided to act.

We are "creator beings" in that how we choose to think and speak creates our reality. Although this creation is a dynamic process, how we think and speak is often governed by belief systems we hold from the past. This creates a pattern that can easily obfuscate the true power we possess to affect our reality. By staying present, we become aware of both our patterns and the power we have to change not only them, but reality itself. *The Navigator Within* contains life-changing formulas that will aid you in harnessing this power.

Each formula has three components: The Insight, *The Intention,* and **The Affirmation.**

The Insight brings us into the present, into self-awareness, where we have a clear view of our thoughts and emotions, and how they affect us. Using self-awareness to change our thinking and interpretations is the first step toward self-empowerment. Only with self-awareness can we penetrate blocks and discord, and expand into our own unlimited potential.

The Intention helps us to focus the mind. What we think about, we attract, and what we focus upon, we become. We have complete control over our focus. When our thoughts are in harmony, we are able to create miracles in our lives.

The Affirmation, when repeated with intention, enters the unconscious mind and becomes a part of our core programming. It is the practical application of the formula. The affirmation is designed to heal the heart and mind by creating a deeper sense of harmony within, and therefore, without.

While reading this book, allow your intuition to guide you. If there are certain affirmations that resonate, repeat and meditate on them throughout the day. The mind can easily become stuck in its old grooves; use the affirmation that applies for a few days to help it transform.

When faced with a quandary, pose a question inside, and open the book. Then find what evokes or validates the best answer for you. You will recognize it by feeling a wave of equanimity and confidence. This is a resource book that you will use again and again.

If there is a formula that you find particularly stirring, do some journaling or free writing. This can often bring clarity to an issue and provide you with an avenue of release.

Feel free to have fun with these formulas! For example—while looking in the mirror, exaggerate your facial expressions and sing the affirmation out loud. You will be amazed at how quickly your mood changes.

We are entering a Golden Age. We stand collectively, on the precipice of great change. Individually, we each play a role in how we affect it. Now is the time to align yourself with the navigator within!

1

As these writings begin, a pregnant moon hangs low in the sky. The leaves on the trees have fallen; a new season has arrived. Change is taking place under the gentle, far-reaching rays of Mt. Shasta. It is available to you, right now, for your healing and transformation.

Simply observe the obsolete anxieties of the past wash through you.

New truths and perceptions are awakening as I enter the zenith of my life, filling it with abundance.

2

Unless a discord is forgotten, it is not forgiven. So long as you remember an injustice or a disturbed feeling, you have forgiven neither the person nor the issue.

Restrain judgments by training your mind to forget everything that is useless or undesirable.

Pouring out unconditional forgiveness puts me in a state of grace within myself.

When forgiveness is complete, my emotional body is serene, happy, kind, and comfortable.

3

Living peacefully with others without judgment is one of the greatest tests of your existence while developing tolerance, compassion, and understanding.

Develop the habit of looking for and finding the best in others and in yourself. Use the discipline of unconditional love and harmony for your own life and for all others.

I no longer judge _______. I now bless them and release them to their highest good.

I release the need to have others conform to my ideas, and I release the habit of judging others and myself.

My life is filled with peace and harmony as I choose to view everyone through the lens of compassion, understanding, and love.

4

Being responsible or being victimized is a choice. Blaming is a way to give your personal power away. Forgiving someone doesn't make right what was done, nor does it endorse continued mistreatment.

Love yourself by setting healthy boundaries and reflecting on how past experiences have strengthened you. This brings gratitude and a softening of the heart, leading to forgiveness.

By honoring my boundaries, I discover empowerment and freedom to move forward in a fuller range of choices.

I surround myself with positive and supportive people.

5

Personal power comes from within and depends upon approval of yourself. Approval comes from integrity and honesty with yourself, which builds strong self-esteem. Strong self-esteem is not vain or arrogant but simply being thankful for who you are.

Maintaining integrity with yourself increases your own personal power by aligning your thoughts, words, and actions.

I am honest with myself and thankful.

6

True love begins by taking care of your physical body as well as keeping your thoughts and feelings positive and loving. Kindness and forgiveness towards yourself and others are the most powerful choices you can make.

Suffer not over what is gone, but celebrate instead what is emerging in life.

I let go of yesterday and tomorrow by embracing each moment with gratitude for the newness of life unfolding.

I lovingly take care of my body, my mind, and my emotions.

7

A great motto to affirm when attached to a certain outcome is, "This or something better is coming my way."

As a Master on the path of Light, if you encounter surprise, disappointment, or hurt, embrace the self-discovery contained in the experience.

I let nothing destructive pass my lips, even in jest.

I express only what is harmonious.

My words are a healing balm.

8

Visibility is the key to authenticity, and authenticity is the doorway to your true self. Nothing is hidden; nothing is denied.

Your soul loves the truth, so acknowledge and tell your truth, and you will experience inner peace.

I maintain the intention to live a life of utter transparency.

9

Your Higher Self brings into your experiences all the shadows you have created. These issues must be looked at in order to make new choices from love and trust, rather than from fear.

Allow your Higher Self to show you your shadows. The shadow is the stuff you don't like about yourself. All your so-called faults, all the things you don't like about yourself, can be your greatest assets. They are simply over amplified, so just turn down the volume. If you deny your greed, you reduce your generosity. If you deny your ugliness, you lessen your beauty.

I forgive myself for being imperfect.

There is nothing within me that I am unwilling to embrace. I accept my strengths and I accept my shadows—by finding the gold in them both.

I embrace my wholeness.

I am free to be me and who I am is enough.

10

God's all-seeing eye acts through light rays, observing and blessing all.

Ask to see everything in the light of God's perfection.

I am made of light, and nourished by the light rays.

My inner core is invincible and indestructible.

I am life in action being molded into eternal perfection.

11

Judging yourself can be turned into an opportunity for releasing that which no longer serves you, and affirming your value instead.

With your free will, choose to release all thoughts and feelings that are not harmonious.

When I catch myself evaluating my performance, I affirm: "I recognize this as judgment and I lovingly release it. I am loved unconditionally, no matter what I am doing. My presence is valuable and in service. I am a flame of Divine love."

12

Merging your free will with the Divine Will is a way to become an Ultimate Human. Therein lies true mastery over the elements.

Visualize yourself becoming shadowless light pouring out golden streams of love that radiate from your heart's center.

My will, and the Divine Will, are one.

13

Discordant thoughts create disintegration and disease in your body. The law of harmony is broken when any kind of irritable or destructive feeling is unleashed.

Choose attention and discipline by not allowing every little disturbing occurrence to color your expression.

When I have negative thoughts, I acknowledge them and release them, but I do not give them expression through my words or deeds.

I create only joyful experiences in my loving world.

14

Thoughts are only activated when you have clothed them with feelings. Discordant feelings destroy your mind and body.

Every thought you think has an effect.

I take charge of my thinking, creating a vibrant body and a peaceful mind.

15

Self-pity, lethargy, and grief come from selfishness, not from love.

Selfishness is making the assumption that everything is about "me."

I choose not to take things personally.

I use my energy to create beauty, harmony, and refinement for myself and others.

16

Are you on a treadmill, or enslaved in service to others?

Never let any desire for service deprive you of time to replenish, time to focus your undivided attention on the "Great Spirit Within."

I operate in the highest realms of dharma—giving the right service and doing the right thing.

I am efficient and balanced.

I replenish myself each day with inspiration.

17

The ego self is on short loan from the Universe and its actions are limited when it is out of touch with its divinity.

Before undertaking a task, invite the Great Spirit within to unleash its wisdom and intelligence in you.

I receive an unlimited supply of courage, strength, power, protection, and guidance.

18

Everyone evolves according to his or her own cycle.

Examine your motivation for helping others. Can you serve with impersonal compassion detached from any outcome? Are you always pleasing others, driven by the yearning for validation and approval?

I am responsible for my own happiness.

I value my own needs and feelings. I help others when my heart is saying yes.

I focus on living my own life lovingly, releasing attachments and expectations.

19

When harmony is maintained, all directions chosen are constructive and build a loving foundation of power.

When noticing discord around you, allow your attention to rest centered in your heart. Breathe fully and notice the spaciousness and a relaxation around the heart.

I maintain inner balance and harmony.

I delete impatience and doubt, as revealed by skepticism, fear, and ridicule.

I am the loving power and the authority in my life.

20

Putting God first helps guide your ego self into a harmonious relationship with life.

In order to receive the blessings of life, conquer the desire to feel inharmoniously, and shut the door to harsh expression.

I let life flow while remaining peaceful, so I may discover fulfillment in living my purpose.

I seek Spirit first, and the material is taken care of.

21

The cosmic law of life is to give; it is in giving of yourself that you expand.

A gift from the heart has no strings or attachment to what might be received back. "Give with love and let go."

Connection with my Higher Self releases me from the vestiges of selfishness and greed.

I am joy expressing itself in life.

22

Be aware of agitating another person's emotions. Doing so will also create havoc in your own life.

Walk gently in dignity, and aspire to be the full expression of the Divine. Walk away from creating or reacting to discord. If a situation needs correction, take time out for clarity. Revisit the situation and simply share what you observed . . . then be silent. Create and encourage well-being in others.

I monitor my expression for harmlessness.

I create tranquility for myself, and tranquility surrounds me.

23

Subtle shadows of rising indignation lead to feeling smug and self-righteous.

Monitor for self-righteousness. Lead unobtrusively, and refrain from forming or offering opinions. You are responsible for the vibration you create. A pebble thrown in the river creates a ripple. In each moment you create a ripple. What is the ripple you are creating?

If invited to give my opinion, I hold the intention for the highest expression and guidance to come forth.

24

Silence and being fully present while listening, open golden doors of opportunity to uplift others.

Remain peacefully silent, and share only when guided to do so.

I vigilantly use my gifts to uplift others with gentleness, fairness, and affection.

25

Stillness, serenity, beauty, and contentment radiate throughout the land.

Each day, take a walk in nature. In your imagination see a grove of evergreens enveloped in the deep silence of falling snow.

I enter the heart of my own solitude, where discord of the evolving ego dissolves.

I bathe in the stillness of Divine Love.

26

One of the most difficult aspects in achieving mastery is to walk the razor's edge between giving and receiving.

When much is received much is required. Constantly receiving and not giving back creates blockage. Giving without receiving chokes abundance. Acknowledge what you have received with gratitude. Find an avenue of expression unique to you to share and pass on a gift in humble gratitude.

I am a master at balancing the knowledge and power I gain from life and giving it back in service.

I give and receive with gratitude.

27

The cosmic Law of Cause and Effect touches everything.

Let go of linear timeline thinking, and visualize wonderful things happening in your life today as a result of your future actions.

Before taking action, I place myself in the other person's shoes and treat him or her the way I would like to be treated.

I respect myself, I respect others, and I honor all life.

28

Feeling enthusiasm creates accomplishments aligned with tenderness and perfection.

Find what makes you experience enthusiasm. Enthusiasm is God expressing through you.

I am enthusiasm.

29

You are not alone, and you are assisted by an unseen, omnipotent symphony.

Achieve liberty and expand your life by setting your mental and feeling world in order.

I am in the right place for the good of all.

I draw around myself individuals for specific purposes—those who endeavor to manifest their own Divine Plan.

I continue to serve, evolve, and make a difference in my circle of influence.

I am never alone; I am always guided by listening to my navigator within.

30

If you focus on your performance, you close heaven's grace. It is never about how you measure your own spiritual altitude.

Concentrate on your desire to uplift in thought, word, and expression. When you compare yourself to others, you fall short. No one in the entire world can do a better job of being you than you.

I am an emissary, a catalyst of inspiration in action and inaction.

I approve of myself so I do not require the approval of others.

I do my best in every moment and then I focus on what is NEXT.

31

Let us break the bonds of cynicism and fear to walk in the sunshine of light, by freeing the intellect and the heart from all distortions in which they have been imprisoned.

Engage with life to inspire and liberate all along the path, in joyous and warmhearted service.

It is safe for me to share my gifts.

I am free to share from my intellect, tailored by the heart.

32

Cultivating a deep heart's desire to understand the motives behind the actions of your colleagues equips you with tolerance and comprehension to hear the deeper cry of their souls. This clarity helps you take actions that result in freedom and support for the highest outcome.

Use the mighty rays of intelligent light. As you place your attention, the streams of light will amplify your capacity to serve through renewed partnership, and heal all you may have injured or been injured by.

I am loved and appreciated for what I am.

I consciously and unconsciously support the highest best in others.

33

The silent criticism of seeing discrepancies and faults in your colleagues disturbs your emotional body and creates reverberating discord within.

Change your vibration by seeing what or whom you have criticized as your ally.

Everything and everyone in the Universe loves and supports me.

I look for and empower the strengths in each person.

34

Organic compassion comes from embracing your feelings. Suppressing or denying feelings ensures they will be acted out unconsciously. The deeper your sorrows have been, the greater your ability to experience joy.

Transcend feelings by letting them be, rather than shutting them out or reacting to them.

I allow emotions to wash through me with solicitous acceptance.

I breathe into and through my feelings in the moment, for they are the juiciness of life.

35

Seeing fear as a friend enables you to transform.

Choose to recognize fear patterns, and shift into a flow of well-being, taking responsibility for expressing your essence in the world in ways that benefit everyone.

I befriend my own successful and troublesome personas by welcoming them into myself.

I face my fears by walking through them, one by one, to gain greater confidence and freedom.

36

Your ability to see what the world needs is a call to greatness.

Explore how you can creatively bring about new ways of doing things that uplift everyone including yourself.

Where imperfection is noticed, I choose to see only opportunity.

37

Harmony is essential to restoration of balance in the body.

Get enough sleep; it provides blessed relief from the bombardment of thoughts and feelings of your mind.

I saturate myself with peace and tenderness, which radiate through my presence to heal any strife.

I love and honor my body; it is my vehicle to experience life.

38

Loving playfulness creates inspired friendship.

Every day, expand in friendship and express creativity to inspire yourself and others.

I commit to playfulness and lovingness.

39

Change your habits and transmutation occurs.

Renew yourself through innovation, or else you will cut a deeper groove into the rut of routine. Be flexible, or you will harden into rigidity.

I am flexible and I let go of self-destructive habits to embrace healthy habits that enhance the quality of life.

40

Embrace your experiences, or shrink and wither away. Reveal your true self, or hide behind your mask.

Look beyond your social mask in order to discover your authentic self. When you are not completely satisfied, happy, healthy, or fulfilling your dreams, therein lies a deception. You have the strength within to face anything and change whatever no longer works for you.

I remember that magnificent oaks from little acorns do grow.

I am in the perfect circumstances for my own evolution.

41

Order in your environment promotes efficiency, peace, and congruence.

Every day, add at least one more element of order in your living or working space, while maintaining all of yesterday's order. Do it now.

I have a place for everything and have everything in its place.

42

Vibrant people are proactive people.

Look for places to go, people to see, and things to do in order to enjoy the flow of heart-connections on a daily basis.

I naturally and actively find ways to connect with others.

43

Where and what you are drawn to is where your light is most beneficial.

Notice the new frequencies and information that are arriving in waves by being fully present in your body and conscious of what you are doing in the moment.

I let go of the old energy patterns of the past.

I am in the right place and in the right circumstances in each moment. Where I am, is where I am most required.

44

It is important to find an avenue to express your talents, gifts, and impulses and to honor your obligation of impersonal service to the Father of Life.

Make a list of the talents and gifts that you have. Find an avenue for this expression in the world. It is most important that you do so.

I am of value and I make a contribution to Life.

With heart and mind surrendering in joy, I offer to serve with no concern for how the claimant is dressed.

45

All of creation seesaws in the balance of giving and receiving.

Harness the power of giving, and work for the greater good.

I am receiving and accepting abundance with lightheartedness.

The more I accept receiving, the more I am able to give.

46

An advanced cycle is in operation, opening new dimensions and possibilities.

Mourn; release what has passed, and awaken to the promise of a new future.

I allow my thoughts to be free. The past is over. I am at peace.

I see what I can birth within my life.

47

Cooperation and patience are highlighted; time is needed to put everything into motion. This is not a time to force the issue or try to move forward aggressively.

Pay attention to details and be ready to integrate your old life with your new life. Settle down to planning without worrying that you are not accomplishing a great deal—the results emerge when the time is right.

I filter everything through my intuitive, spiritual, and inspirational focus.

I am patient; I treat each situation as a work of art in progress.

48

This is a time for teamwork and building relationships that will benefit you in the future, a time to improve your ability to work with others productively.

To have a friend, you must be a friend, so be calm, cool, and pleasant. Look for the people you want to deepen bonds with, and focus on doing that.

I naturally cultivate inspirational friendships.

I am present to life and contribute back to life with others, harmoniously.

49

In order to have a thing, you must first give it.

Whatever good you want, decree that everyone is given this blessing and your fulfillment is hastened.

Right now, I see, hear, and feel that everyone is being given the blessing of ____________________ (fill in the blank).

I support the highest gifts and talents in others. In doing so, the highest gifts and talents manifest naturally for me.

50

The Vedas and Kashmir tapestry were woven in patient dexterity, kindness, gratitude, and perfection. If even one thread was woven with the energy of intolerance, unkindness, or discord, it was not accepted in the Master's house. Even if a thread is perfect, with the most brilliant design, it will not survive if created with negative energies of turbulence and ingratitude.

Patiently create a master tapestry of your life with love, kindness, gratitude, and peace.

I step forth to express and create a master tapestry of love with my own mix of healing expression in the world.

51

The fires of purification bring you new life.

Welcome the emerging flames that will be followed with new growth so that life blossoms.

Like the ancient Phoenix, legendary bird of resurrection sacrificed in the fires of life, I am now awake to a new life and new frequencies within.

I surrender to the blaze; it consumes the destructive aspects of my personality.

52

You are at a fork in the road. You can continue on the same path and perpetuate the difficult and trying events of the past, or you can choose a different path—one that involves risk and possible failure, but introduces positive, revitalizing changes that enhance your life with new promise, purpose, and achievements.

Dare to take a new path. There are no failures, just a discovery of what works and what doesn't in your life. You can choose again.

I commit to following the path of change. If I falter, I simply forgive myself, say "I recommit," and continue on.

I am courageous and indomitable. I move forward with ease and grace.

53

This is a time in which to experience soul growth and to give of your time, talents, and insights. Intuition will be humming this year with revelation, vision, and illumination. There will be opportunities to gain prominence or be in the limelight, in a favorable position to launch a new product or service. Definitely a "Go for it" year!

Pay close attention to your intuition as to where you give of your time and talents.

I trust my vision to clearly guide me in embracing new opportunities.

I trust and listen to my own intuition. As I do so, more inner guidance comes.

54

Leaders render great service to the Universe and to their fellow man while attempting, at the same time, to work out their individual karmas. If Leaders waited until they were perfect before sharing their knowledge and light, we would have no representation in the world of form.

Consider Leaders as fellow students upon the path. Bless them, pray for them, and love them for their courage to take on the karma of other individuals through such service. Raise Leaders by your love. Do not destroy them with condemnation, silent or spoken.

I see perfection emerging in each Leader.

I am a leader living my life with integrity, kindness, and light-heartedness.

55

Your heart, not a sense of duty, must prompt you whether to use your energies in collective endeavors or to attempt to ascend the spiritual path alone. You can shun cooperative endeavors in order to find personal peace, or you can join in to serve a cause that gives spiritual strength of united energies for the good of the whole.

Be a magnet for spiritual guidance and inspiration.

I ask that the will of God be done for me, through myself and through the people I interact with.

I am a walking inspiration.

56

Buds on a lilac tree open to release a sweet fragrance, which is their gift to the Universe. They never try to possess or control their fragrance. To release is the natural order in the Universe.

Enjoy the art of your creations in the moment and then . . . let go.

I naturally release my gifts for the good of the Universe.

57

As the wings of the dove glide into the blue sky, freedom is manifest—in Beingness.

Remember that no matter how things appear, the Light of God never fails.

I am always free to be, and free to be me.

I am enough—just as I am.

58

Gratitude is a feeling that changes the quality of vibration and creates light and harmony all around you. It is not enough to be grateful in your mind. A grateful feeling heart creates a happy mind and a healthy body, and adds to the light of the world.

Consciously endeavor to be grateful through your feelings, where greater portions of your energies reside.

I love feeling the waves of gratitude.

59

When your plans unexpectedly develop a hiccup in them, it is time to go with the flow and trust. Sunny days will soon arrive.

Reflect upon the marvel of the invisible hands of intervention and orchestration to bring nourishment, blessings, and healings.

I trust as I surrender to the current . . . to embrace the perfection of the Universe unfolding around me.

60

New forms of expression will manifest, bringing creativity, laughter, camaraderie, and spiritual growth as you embark on the path ahead.

It is time to resurrect parts of your life, to release any fears, and to invite regenerating changes.

I accept the refreshing newness of life that is available to me now.

61

Invoking the Divine purifies your consciousness of any discord.

Consciously sustain harmony within, so that transmuted impurities are not replaced by the destructive use of free will.

I call upon the powers of the Sacred Fire to remove the core and causes of disharmony that jeopardize Personal Mastery.

62

You are not meant to suffer while assisting and inspiring others along their spiritual path; suffering is just a man-made law.

Realize that suffering is not necessary for growth.

It is my divine right to inspire joyously.

I am joyous inspiration.

63

It is wise to take three days to decide yes or no on a commitment.

Reflect on what a prospective commitment would involve. What is the emotional impact, and what does it encompass?

I take time in making solid decisions that support my spiritual growth and overall well-being. If on the third day I feel a slight sting, or the heart says no and the mind says yes, the answer is "No."

I say "no" easily and graciously.

I say "yes" gently and confidently.

64

You have been a hard-working gardener, planting many seeds along the way. The Universe has nourished these seeds; they have blossomed and are now full of rich fruit.

In your thoughts, words, and feelings, bless the fruit of your labor with gratitude. It is time to collect your harvest.

I am ready and worthy to accept the harvest that the Universe abundantly provides.

65

The passport to freedom is to watch your motives, which stimulate your endeavors. Are you being authentic with yourself or are you driven? Driven behavior becomes repetitive, limited satisfaction; joyless martyrdom; and perfectionism. An authentic choice feels right and is deeply satisfying with no guilt, exhaustion, resentment or loss of interest.

Be guided by humility, discrimination, and the honesty of introspection. Allow time to contemplate; keeping so busy that you never have to think doesn't work. Examining your motives for doing what you do will allow you to hear your inner truth, which leads to wisdom and doing what's authentic for you.

I am self-awareness and my inner wisdom guides me.

I create a peaceful presence around myself; anyone who crosses my path receives blessings.

66

Life is at its best when love, money, and creativity grow in harmony.

Ask yourself these three questions: How much love and abundance am I willing to allow? How am I getting in my own way? Am I willing to consider the possibility of consistently feeling good and having things go well in my life all the time?

I allow love and abundance to flow freely in my life.

I am willing to accept feeling happy all the time.

67

Fear is excitement without the breath.

Get out of the fog of fear, and transform it into the clarity of exhilaration. Take nice, easy, deep breaths—and just go for it.

I am in charge of the exhilaration, and I go for it! It is most important that I do so.

I feel the fear and just move through it, step by step.

68

Have fun while learning, and creativity with skill will follow.

Make time to hear "the still, small voice within." For now, be patient, and continue doing what you are doing. Thus you create a strong foundation for your ventures to develop.

I have fun while patiently learning and creating strong foundations for my ventures.

69

Removing selfish motives will result in having freedom and receiving all the assistance you require in the fulfillment of your heartfelt goals.

Examine your motives for service to mankind. What is your motive for sharing your knowledge and experiences? Are you sharing for the purpose of expanding and supporting a fellow traveler's choices, or is it to build up your ego's spiritual pride?

I request removal of the causes and core of selfish motives in my life, in order to become the manifest expression of the Divine.

I monitor my expression and empower heartfelt goals.

70

Home is a state of continued, uninterrupted harmony inside of you. Home is where feelings, thoughts, memories, spoken words, and actions are in complete harmony with Spirit and fellow man.

Choose to maintain an uninterrupted harmony with the physical, mental, emotional, and spiritual bodies.

From a position of uninterrupted harmony, I radiate and send forth blessings to all, with no thought of self-acclaim.

I am a blessing to life.

71

You are either ascending or descending, according to where you allow your attention to flow.

Be vigilant about freeing yourself from the mass consciousness of fear, anger, and imperfection that surround you.

From moment to moment, I am choosing the energy that I allow to enter into my thoughts, feelings, and actions.

I change the quality of energy around me, changing shadows into light through my awareness and attention.

72

The power to think creates form. The power to feel fills that form with life.

Examine carefully the motive behind the idea or thought pattern entertained. Is it selfless and beneficial to all of life?

With clarity, I energize my visions with enthusiasm.

73

Using your imagination to create beauty, your wildest dreams manifest. You CAN do it, for God is with you!

Be the catalyst for others in manifesting their creative abilities.

I assist in clearing the path for the ultimate destiny of every life stream to express its unique song.

74

Actions are balanced and controlled according to the requirements of the moment. This is mastery.

Be anchored in the heart.

Beloved Mighty Presence of God, please guide me in taking the noblest action for my possessions and surroundings while honoring the resources that you have entrusted in my care for the highest outcome for all.

I am loving wisdom in action.

75

Openness, kindness, and charity in listening anchor your awareness in your heart; thus, it becomes easier to communicate with others. If there is too much of a self-centered attitude, then fear, doubt, and suspicions result, your heart shuts down, and it is very difficult to communicate with others.

The truth sets you free. Be at liberty to speak your truth gently and set your own boundaries.

I expand in love, abundance, and success each day, as I inspire those around me to do the same.

I release assumptions and ask for clarity in my communications.

I let go of my agenda to become fully present when listening to another.

76

A seed planter lovingly plants seeds of new possibilities. Some people dream of changing their lives. The question is, do they really want to change, or are they in resistance? If they just want someone to sympathize with them or carry them along, hoping that will be enough . . . it won't work.

Bless and release others by honoring their choices. If they earnestly want to change, a seed planter will come and sow the seeds for new growth.

I am peaceful and comfortable with who I am, and with who others choose to be.

77

You have the ability to read another person's energy with your inner eye.

When you find that you are repulsed by what is visually or verbally coming towards you, stay centered in your heart and send out blessings while repeating the mantra, "This is your lesson, not mine." This keeps any distorted energy from affecting your emotional field.

I trust my divine guidance and the Higher Self that protects me.

78

Anger, denial, and clutching to the past will not alter the new image that is emerging. Old friends pass away; new friends appear like the night giving birth to a new day.

Evolution sets its own pace; trust and allow this transformation to gently unfold. A richer tapestry is coming to light.

I welcome new friends into my life.

I willingly surrender to change and the new image emerging.

Everything happens for the best.

79

Amethyst jewels magnetize, radiate, and anchor the heart in beauty and perfection. Where the shadows are the greatest, the Violet Ray of light is required the most.

Call forth the Light to blaze up, around, and through the murkiness—transmutation creates freedom, peace, and harmony.

May all fear of self-discipline be removed as I embrace JOY.

80

When falling asleep or awakening, are your thoughts re-creating ill feelings? Is your mind habitually circling around imaginary scenarios that spiral downward?

Let go of the old appearances of lack, ill health, and discord of any kind.

I am loved and cherished, and I send forth support for the highest outcome.

The past is dissolved and cleared, having been set free from bygone imperfections.

81

The exterior mirrors the interior, and the interior is reflected in the exterior.

Listen to the silence between the birds singing; notice the soothing calm and contentment within. See the morning light reflected on the leaves of the trees; nourishment and wisdom are activated. Hear the gurgling stream flowing eastward; cleansing and clearing are complete.

As I reflect on the beauty and perfection of nature, I am cleansed within and filled with contentment.

I am peace. I am contentment.

82

Awareness plus risk-taking equals growth. Unhappiness and stagnation result when you are aware that something is not working in your life but are afraid to make the needed changes; change will lead to something better. New growth and enthusiasm result from taking the risk of implementing change through awareness. This brings advancement and places you on the path of living your purpose.

Think about your choices: Would you like to be stuck and secure in the mire of discord, or free and versatile as a hummingbird seeking nectar? Choose something to change that has not been working in your life, and take the risk to transform it now.

I am aware of what the changes are that will lead to better things in my life.

I enthusiastically embrace the changes that I require in order to grow.

I bravely take risks, which enable me to live my purpose.

83

Your old fears and blocks in self-expression have been cleared. When doubt creeps in, you can affirm, "No! That block has been transmuted and is gone."

Remember the motto, "Everyone and everything in the Universe loves and supports me."

It is safe for me to share my gifts.

I am loved and appreciated for who and what I am.

I am capable.

84

To be a comfort and healing presence to others, use discernment in what to share.

By listening holistically and observing others' actions, see how willfully invested and committed they are to their chosen viewpoints. Ask yourself, "Would the sharing of my experiences create turbulence or be uplifting and supportive for them to hear?"

My words are divinely guided to heal and comfort others.

85

There are multiple paths leading to the same destination. You have chosen a direct path. Your friend may have chosen to take a longer, winding course. You both have a choice and a destiny to follow.

Keep your vision on your destination, while maintaining tolerance and patience with others who cross your path.

I make wise choices for myself, and I honor the choices that others make for themselves.

86

Self-Mastery is the only Mastery there is.

Take time daily for self-assessment.

Introspection and retrospection help me use self-knowledge and apply it with enthusiasm in my own life.

87

The more you approve of yourself and do what you love doing, the more others will accept you. By setting off in a new direction and living creatively, you can take bold steps while breathing through the fears that arise.

Overcome your trepidation by moving forward one step at a time. As a result, you will develop confidence, manifest success, and serve as a role model for those around you.

By following my own inspiration courageously, I discover no real obstacles in my way, and I ride the new currents with smoothness and poise.

88

Now is the time to build on feelings of balance, harmony, and kindness so that you may be of service in times of stress and turmoil.

Take a real or imaginary walk amongst some pine trees to inhale the fragrance of their healing elixir. This aroma repairs the invisible fissures in your emotional body and clears old guilt and anxieties.

I maintain a steady state of balance and harmony so that I may be of service to others.

89

Taking time for contemplation gives rise to discernment and understanding. Contemplation of truth brings illumination, illumination brings peace, and peace brings mastery.

All paths are points of truth. Be at Peace.

I am at peace.

My inner state is a stabilizing power in my home, community, nation, and on the Earth itself.

90

The trough follows the crest of a wave. In the flow of your life, value both action and inaction. It is the inaction and rest from which you draw wisdom, light, and blessings.

Every three months, have a week of solitude or go someplace that nourishes your soul. To truly nourish and serve others, you must first nourish yourself.

Periods of lull to contemplate and reflect bring insights that move you forward in balanced action, stepping higher on the pathway of life.

I am taking time to replenish my spirit.

91

The creative force of the Universe—the Threefold Trinity of the Heart—guides the light substance. The light essence obeys and becomes the clothing of my own creative flame.

Visualize Divine Light dancing in your heart.

The Divine Flame works its magic within me to carry me onward and forward.

92

The intrinsic drive to serve God can get befuddled. When you rush in to serve the limited need of an individual, you receive back only the gift that the imperfect can offer. If nothing is received for the service, discouragement and bitterness can follow.

Remember to dedicate your service to and for the Creator, detaching and letting go of expectation or anticipation of reward, and you will be free to celebrate each creative endeavor.

I serve God by serving others.

I support and empower the highest qualities in another.

93

Creative expression, once completed, is your gift and offering to God. Ownership is no longer needed, as the gift is in God's hands. The way in which the gift is used in the bigger picture remains undisclosed.

Focus on bravely engaging to express your gifts, letting go, and experiencing freedom and joy in the Now . . .

Creative expression in the moment is what I revel in.

94

The time for clearing is now; not getting rid of what isn't working in your life limits the manifestation of your highest capabilities. A tree keeps growing; when it stops growing it dies. Just like a tree, choose to keep growing and living fully.

Expanded vision includes developing your inherent Divinity. On the escalator going up, consciously take the next step, giving maximum expression to the wholeness you are, while honoring your body, heart/mind bond, and beatifying spirit.

I choose to externalize the highest possible expression of God—the perfection that is within.

95

The center of power is released through the spoken word. When your heart, consciousness, and sub-conscious mind come into complete resonance, then one spoken word brings manifestation. In the past, focusing on your flaws solidified their destructive influence in your living experience and robbed you of your power.

One affirmation from your lips will not reverse decades of distorted beliefs and expressions. Through clear repetitive affirmations, you can drive into them a positive radiation. In time, these negative energies from your past will be transmuted into patterns of perfection and fulfillment in your future.

Closely monitor what comes out of your mouth. Requalify this energy and call forth your true divine qualities to blaze up through and shatter those patterns created by carelessly spoken words.

I AM:

Strong when I take adversity and teach it to smile.

Brave when I jump in and just do it.

Loving when I embrace my shadow and my light, acknowledging my wholeness.

Wise when I creatively play with what the Universe presents.

Alive to tomorrow's possibilities more than yesterday's false steps.

Free to follow what gives my spirit joy.

Powerful when my love overcomes the love of power.

Honorable when I respect and honor myself and, therefore, others more fully.

Happy when I smell lavender, and thankful for the blessing.

Gracious when I forgive in others the faults I condemn in myself.

Independent when I control myself with no need to control others.

Rich when I am grateful for what I have.

Beautiful when I am at peace with myself.

96

In the past you may have run on the periphery of life, shouting the hollow sounds that resounded nowhere but in your own ears. The requirement and reverence for silence is now exquisite.

Be silent with your tongue, peaceful in your emotional field, and free of fruitless thinking. The most challenging step is to be still, to have the inward patience to hear the Voice of Silence.

Listening to the Voice of Silence, I let go of my mental and emotional agenda and receive illumination.

I am stillness while in action.

97

Uninterrupted harmony is essential for new creations. If you find your mind condemning something outside yourself, you have not mastered it within yourself. With awareness, you can transmute discord by placing your attention on the light of harmony.

Call on and insist upon unbroken harmony in your life. No person, place, condition or thing will be strong enough to destroy this harmony.

I create and experience peaceful and loving scenarios.

98

The most marvelous investment is to awaken good feelings wherever you are. The burden of the world is lightened whenever and wherever you create harmony. You can harmoniously scrub the floor, or do your work in a state of resentment and anger. Constructive and symmetrical energy is a natural expression of the Divine.

Create harmony in everything you do, and above all within you. To be in harmony with yourself, start with answering these three questions: Who do you pretend to be? Who are you afraid you are? Lastly, who are you? If you examine what you don't want others to know about you, you will discover the false assumptions or self-doubts that motivate how you pretend to be or show up in the outer world.

Your core is who you really are. It is where your wisdom and divinity resides.

I am willing to release my self-doubts.

I am my inner core, which is always harmonious.

My freedom is ensured when I exude energy that is harmonious.

I am harmony, in everything I do.

99

Spirituality is a state of "Being," a state of consciousness that brings you back to the awareness of Love, Light, and Divinity. It is not the Dos or Don'ts or the many rules you have imposed on yourself. Like a dove gliding in the sky, freedom is not so much in doing but in "Being."

Let go of your fears by surrendering to what is and releasing judgments concerning how situations "should" be.

I open my heart with Love and Trust.

I surrender to change with willing acceptance; it will deliver me from the chains I've created from the past.

The universe is a loving and benevolent place, and provides everything for me when I trust.

I am here for the purpose of evolving my consciousness and gaining greater mastery.

100

"Listening Grace" occurs when all the restless parts of you are still; then the beauty, grace, blessings, and presence of the Great Spirit are revealed. Listening Grace affords you opportunities that come in split seconds; if you are busy sending out thought waves, you miss the incoming currents carrying illumination, benedictions, and blessings.

In silence, every day, let your soul and consciousness rest within a field of reverent love.

I am safe and I am secure.

I connect with my inner presence by living in the Now moment, which holds the agenda of my soul.

I establish a state of grace by harmonizing my "many selves."

I stop sending out requests and become present to silence, allowing grace to reveal itself.

101

Speak only words of respect and harmony.

If you are not sure how to communicate without offending, go to your heart, take a deep breath and say, "I now communicate from a loving heart, invoking the illumination and wisdom imprinted within for the perfect expression to come forth."

I pause before speaking and ask myself—is it honest, is it kind, is it necessary?

I am creating through my expression, which is multiplied and returned lovingly to me.

102

Life becomes difficult only when you ignore the prompting of your soul.

Choose to understand your life's lessons, and remove the shackles of illusion and separation.

As I awaken and come into balance, there is one less burden on a world that is in desperate need of many kinds and levels of healing.

I examine the obstacles that arrive in my life, directing me to go in an unknown direction. I trust, surrender, and work with the promptings of the Universe. It always leads to the best circumstances in the long run.

I am empowered and wiser by each challenge I overcome.

103

Yesterday, the word "love" was categorized and defined as being an emotion or sentimentality. Today, the word love signifies a state of Being—in harmony with yourself and with your surroundings, offering absolution and inspiration.

Begin to love and approve of yourself and release all guilt and self-punishment. The more you embrace yourself, the greater container within develops for accepting others as they are.

I love myself. I am at peace with myself. My expression is harmonious.

I am compassionate with myself.

104

By sitting quietly and placing your awareness on your breath, you become centered in the Now moment. There is no pondering of the past or peering into the future; being in the Now moment, you are in the continuous uninterrupted flow of divine love.

Choose to be more aware of where you place your attention.

I am fully present—right here, right Now—I am awareness.

My breath centers me in the Now moment.

105

Your internal guidance acts sometimes as a brake and other times as an accelerator, assisting every evolutionary step to be taken "at the right time and place." If you are forcing your spiritual growth, your soul may slow the pace by introducing obstacles in your way. Likewise, if you resist being true to your power, love, and wisdom, your soul will support you while your armored identity dissolves.

Listen to and align with divine guidance; then grace and ease will be experienced in the flow of life's constant changes.

My Higher Self is the captain of my life. I am thus an empowered team player with my life's divine director at the helm, not a pawn victimized by outside forces.

I can choose to feel betrayed when my limited identity is collapsing or I can trust that my soul is liberating me.

I am in the flow of life, experiencing it with ease and grace.

106

By changing yourself, you change the world.

Feel emotions without judgment or reactivity, using the tools of appreciation and forgiveness to reclaim innocence. Experience courage and hope by living in the coherent patterns of love, regardless of the outer chaos. Change your perception and your world changes.

I am guided by my inner life and in charge of how I show up in the world.

I am accountable for myself and for the impact I make in my surroundings.

I embrace everything in life and shrink from nothing.

I am calm in the center of a storm.

107

Empowerment and enthusiasm arise from embracing the unexpected and using the inner eye of imagination to give birth to something beneficial. In this process, you open to the presence of God, entering through a thinly veiled doorway into the higher dimensions of love and possibilities.

Place your attention on creating what is inspiring for you with each circumstance the Universe presents.

I embrace life's unexpected moments and use them as a doorway to my deeper expansion and creative expression.

I use my imagination to birth what is beneficial.

108

You cannot see into the depths of a river unless the surface is perfectly calm.

Access a fuller range of creativity through wise passivity—the capacity to allow the mind to become still each day.

I allow my mind to rest. I am still like the mountain.

I am the inner core that is steady, grounded, and invincible.

109

Belief or lack of belief is unimportant; what matters is direct experience.

Trust in your ineffable experience and bathe in the peace that bypasses all understanding.

I trust and treasure my own moments of inner illumination.

110

We are an interwoven Universe of Oneness. Water is vapor, liquid, or solid, yet always the one compound of hydrogen and oxygen, as are stars, planets, rocks, plants, animals, and humans—the essence of One Great Spirit.

When looking at something small, see the infinite in it. A grain of sand is part of the shoreline. A drop of water is part of the ocean, not separate.

I am part of Great Spirit.

I am connected to everything and everyone.

111

A mystic's love is the total dedication of one's own will, the deep-seated desire and tendency of the soul towards its Source.

Your spirit also requires nourishment. Explore different spiritual paths to see what resonates and is alive with direct experience for you. In all things acknowledge Source and your path becomes directed and blessed. Trust and explore.

I am loved, supported, and guided in my search for Truth.

I surrender to the greater will of Divine Source.

I am loved regardless of the pace I choose on my journey with Source.

112

Pure awareness is the underlying reality of waking, dreaming, and dreamless sleep.

Perceive the world through your heart instead of your mind.

I am more than my thoughts, feelings, and body sensations.

I am that I am, I am that I am, I am that I am . . .

113

One who has achieved enlightenment sees the Self present in everything. In this state of awareness, there can be no "second," and hence no fear. The Spirit is beyond suffering and fear. One who knows this has found peace and is the master of one's self, exuding endurance with calm concentration and seeing the spirit in All—The Spirit of the Universe.

See the Universe and yourself as One.

I am One with The Spirit of the Universe.

114

The challenge on the path of Mastery is choosing between listening to the thoughts of the mind or following the heart.

Follow your heart, even if it guides you to take a sharp turn into unfamiliar terrain.

I am in charge of my thoughts. I choose to redirect my thoughts to rest in the heart.

115

It is time to train your mind to dwell on beauty and thoughts that uplift others.

Pay attention to your mind, as it habitually hovers on imaginary discord.

Oh Angelic and Divine Master, help cleanse the old conditioned habits of my mind and assist me to anchor the new healing rays of light. Bring in the books, places, and people I require to assist in the transformation to a New Earth.

When in an imaginary scenario of discord, I consciously stop and redirect the imaginary scenario into what I would like to experience instead.

I am a blessing and I am a blesser to life.

116

Materialism is the old paradigm. The Law of Attraction is not designed to manifest material possessions or fulfill greedy, selfish desires.

When you find yourself focusing on future events in a negative way, redirect your attention on the positive. What is it you require?

I align with the broader agenda of my Higher Self in the use of the Law of Attraction. I intend to harness its power to claim inner abundance and to support the practice of higher states of consciousness.

I invite the inner abundance to flow through me into my world.

117

Winter has arrived; in silent stillness, snowflakes descend lightly, resting and covering the land. The moon and stars are hidden, while iridescence from the snow radiates Light everywhere in the night. The dawn gradually sheds pinkish golden hues across the White Mountain. Magic is in the air, with the promise of the Ancients to soon be revealed.

Imagine snowflakes whirling in delight upon Mt. Shasta, where Heaven joins Earth. Listen to the spacious silence of the descending snow, rest in the temple within, absorbing gentleness—merging—I AM.

Witness the presence of love and potential in the midst of ordinary life.

I notice the glow of contentment and an undercurrent of indomitable assurance within.

I have come through the seasons and now my soul is free to experience Victory.

I invite the magic and mystery to reveal itself to me.

118

It is your responsibility to monitor your thoughts, which affect your feelings. If your thoughts are uplifting, then your feelings are balanced.

Whenever you check the time, also check your thoughts. Pause to take a slow, relaxed breath and ask yourself, "What were my thoughts dwelling on?" Redirect them as required. Thoughts can spiral you downward into discord or upward into gratitude and balance.

When I practice harmony within, it flows into my outer surroundings.

My goal is to be harmonious at all times and it starts with my thoughts.

I am not my thoughts or feelings, I am more than this.

119

Darkness cloaks the early morning light with a silent benevolence. All that is required is to accept this blanket of quiet peace and stillness, absorbing its gift of tranquility.

Breathe in peace and stillness; imagine peace filling every cell of your body.

Within my mind and heart, I commune in gratitude for the bounty provided to produce the greatest happiness for myself and those around me and to accomplish the greatest success in all I do.

I am benevolence.

120

Piercing heaven's blue, Mt. Shasta's argent image sits in obscured grandeur, a silent sentinel, luminous and transcendent. God's sublime handiwork invokes purity of heart, divine insight, and serenity for all.

Picture Mt. Shasta in your imagination. See the falling snow descending softly and silently. Become the silence . . .

I allow the tranquility of the great mountain to speak to me and inspire me with insights.

I am willing to transform and transcend my limitations.

I am purity. I am serenity.

121

Discernment is a way of making life choices without judging them as good or bad.

With love, simply release an old way of being as a flavor of the truth that no longer resonates with you in this moment.

I release places, people, and situations to their highest good.

I release guilt and the compulsive "I have to . . ." I now gravitate to that which resonates with me.

I am discernment. I do what is uplifting and release anything that spirals me downward. I can choose again.

I love and respect myself. I surround myself with innovative friends and inspirational opportunities that resonate with me.

122

A formulated idea or creed is a static thing, never changing.

Never let your thoughts harden into "this is the only way," locking in place a rigid concept as a perceived truth.

I dedicate my life to Change; all past beliefs, sacred as they may have been, are sacrificed to the expanded consciousness of now.

I release my opinions, the beliefs of how things should be, or having to be right.

I allow all flavors of the Truth, for they are but guideposts along the path.

I stay open to following the gentle nudges of Source from moment to moment.

I am flexible flowing easily and gracefully with change.

123

As the leaf relies on the twig, the twig on the branch, the branch on the limb, the limb on the trunk, and the trunk on the root, secure in Mother Earth, you are part of the grand design of the Universe, secure within the indefinable—God.

Relax into the knowing that your place in the Universe is secure.

I need not "be" anything; to simply "be" is enough. I am part of a Universal Design.

124

The greatest quest is to conquer and transmute your ignorance, selfish ambitions, and desire for recognition by extinguishing your willfulness.

In the smallest to the grandest of plans, remember always that what you set into motion reverberates back to you through the Universal Law: As you sow, so do you reap.

Being accountable and mastering myself floods my soul with peace.

I am guided by kind intentions.

I release the willfulness of rigidity and tunnel vision to stay open to possibilities.

I create and plant seeds of generosity, sowing abundance.

125

Your actions are off kilter and in darkness if your ego-self is the sole power in charge. You do not know, until many eons pass through the back door of time, what about your past is concealed in the great book of records. The circular veil of time now extends an invitation to enter through the front door of a Golden Dimension.

Right the injustices and pardon the injuries of the past.

Spirit guides my actions, directing them toward harmony and divine motivation.

I am Golden Healing Light.

126

A Master Healer is one who creates space for others to feel safe enough to heal themselves and find their own way Home.

Emotional clearing strengthens your personal balance, allowing you to stand firm in your own power and contribute back to society.

As I remain open to the removal of blocks within my own emotional body, I become more benevolent and beneficial in my circle of influence.

I am safety and strength in a storm.

I am presence in listening and being. There is nothing else required.

127

This is a time for creative expression, and acting as a catalyst for transformation. Ideas, plans, or projects started years ago will now progress and provide a new basis for action.

Let go of hearsay, preconceived ideas, and judgments. Just go for it. If the experience is uplifting and empowering, it's a yes. If it's draining and makes you feel bad, you walk away. Trust in your power of discrimination as you explore. Try something new and give yourself the experience and you might find yourself doing a 360-degree shift in perspective to evolve, being enriched and empowered.

I value freedom, beauty, and authenticity. I am a catalyst for change.

Adopting an attitude of what I can contribute, rather than what I can get in a situation, helps move me forward.

I am willing to expand my comfort zone by allowing myself to experience the projects that I am drawn to.

I am a catalyst for uplifting creations. I am free to explore what is interesting and draws my full attention.

128

We all are on a ladder climbing up one rung at a time. Competing with another person on the ladder creates imbalance and strife, teetering the ladder or causing it to topple. Competition reflects a core belief in the concept of lack. Each one of us is needed; each person plays a role in keeping the ladder balanced and anchored.

No one has to lose for you to win. Abundance is the signature of the Universe. As you support another person's success, your own success is assured. Competition brings separation and isolation, while cooperation multiplies success and unites.

I play my part in the symphony of life, knowing that all individuals are needed to create perfect harmony.

I co-create with collaboration, cooperation, and celebration.

129

A gyroscope spins without being affected by the tilting of its mount in any direction. If what you are constantly doing or thinking is pulling you out of balance, chances are you are hanging on to a way of being that no longer serves your highest good. You are like a spinning top seeking its own balance.

Hanging on to wishes of the past or a worn out way of being, blocks you from moving forward. Release what no longer serves or inspires you.

I am free to move in any direction chosen. I am balanced.

130

Your focus is always the blueprint for your future.

Seek guidance and validation rather than answers.

I instantly perceive answers from within for what I am required to know.

Validation is swiftly seen as I move forward, walking and living my truth from within.

I envision what I wish to fulfill.

My focus triggers manifestation in my life.

131

The more you trust your intuition, the more guidance you will receive.

If you catch yourself trying to "analyze away" what your intuition tells you is happening, remember that there is a higher plan in operation.

I respect and trust my intuition, even when it disagrees with what I think I want.

I let go of relying on others for guidance. I trust my own intuition.

132

Cornucopia is the horn of plenty. The Goddess Fortuna carries a horn overflowing with golden shimmering coins. By invitation, she arrives with her radiant beauty, purity, and wisdom to assist in manifesting abundance. Liberation and Ascension are assured as you share your cornucopia of innate gifts and talents while feeling much appreciation and deep thankfulness.

Open the doors wide for Fortuna's entrance as she brings overflowing creativity, good fortune, and spiritual and material wealth. Blaze into and annihilate ignorance and unconscious beliefs in lack and limitation.

With humble gratitude, I accept all the gifts from the Lady of Luck.

I am thankfulness. I expand in the heart of Gratitude.

133

The creative power of God is far greater than your feelings of self-doubt and unworthiness.

By the Great Central Sun, earnestly invite into your consciousness ideas, patterns, forms, designs, and wisdom of Universal Law to manifest in full expression in your life now.

May the golden-ruby rays wash away self-doubt and shine through me in harmonious beauty to bless the people, the animals, and the elementals.

I am worthy. I am free to manifest my full creative expression.

134

Laughter is the most powerful tool for healing, as it penetrates all walls of defense. Humor changes the vibration of a situation and brings lightheartedness. In a moment of deep laughter, the debilitating energies of fear and worry are suspended.

The ability to laugh at yourself brings self-mastery. It brings your inner child, adolescent, and adult into communion, uniting them as one. Humor and laughter break up cycles of despair and free you to mobilize your own inner resources.

Humor triggers the creative side of your brain. It is often in hindsight that you see the humor in a serious or difficult scenario. Sharing of our universal foibles and laughing at our own gaffes builds community.

Surrender to the heavenly impulse of laughter; ride the waves of mirth in abandonment. Apply the gift of laughter, for living with the imperfections of life.

Use humor to face adversity, accessing joy in absurdity.

Practice positive healing humor by laughing with, not at, another. When in doubt, ask permission to share your form of humor so as not to offend.

Laughing at life raises my spirits and brings me into alignment.

I allow divine laughter to convulse through my mind and body, cleansing me and transforming negative emotions into vibrancy.

I choose to find humor in every situation by seeing upsets as opportunities to laugh.

I look for and create laughter in each moment, as "too much of a good thing can be wonderful."

135

Bring a thing to pass and you'll see it in the looking glass.

Reflect on the mirror that is mirrored back to you through the people in your life. Gently embrace the aspects you dislike in others as hidden aspects of yourself. Once these aspects are recognized and acknowledged, they no longer have the power to sabotage your life.

I embrace my beauty, strengths, and flaws through acceptance versus judgment. All aspects are balanced and tapered for the requirements of the moment.

I restore harmony and tranquility wherever I pass.

I look into the mirror and see God dwelling within you and me.

136

The people around you are part of your Greater Self, awakening to their true identity.

If you cannot be a great big star, then be a candle in the corner where you are.

I develop my talents to their highest potential while assisting others in fulfilling their life's mission.

I am light wherever I am. Each light is vital.

137

What is the covenant you made with the Universe regarding your existence in the here and now?

It is time to Awaken and play your part in the birthing of a new era. A covenant is unbreakable.

I walk the earth manifesting my divine creative potential.

I choose to awaken and honor my contract with the Universe.

Every small act done with integrity matters and it is most important that I do it!

138

What is the quality or motive that drives your ambition? Destructive influences are driven by self-interest, guided by pride and greed. Constructive influences are fueled by the love for life, helpful and generous.

Let clarity and humility be the guiding pillars for the expression of your ambition.

Oh Lord, purify and harmonize my mental and emotional body so that I may be a catalyst in raising consciousness while emitting gentle peace.

Tough Love is sometimes the Love that is required, by withdrawing support of destructive habits.

I generously support constructive habits that empower life.

I am crystal clarity, doing what is most beneficial in each moment.

139

Many people accept that life is hard and difficult. Actually, this is not true. Once you learn to direct your thinking towards positive solutions and use your spirit in day-to-day life, all problems seem to vanish like fog surrendering to the sunshine.

Luck is a self-created state, caused by doing the right thing for the right reason while in a harmonious state of mind. The process of maintaining a state of mind that produces luck in life can be learned and used by anyone. Once the balance of spirit and the material world is understood and your ego is well managed, then a rich life of continued happiness is yours.

Maintain inner harmony with your thoughts and focus on positive outcomes and solutions.

I draw forth now, in this lifetime, all the spiritual gifts I have developed over all my incarnations to help conquer any unconscious unworthiness.

I draw on my full divine knowledge to be used in congruous service while doing the right thing and for the right reason.

I flow easily and happily with the currents of life while listening to divine guidance.

I am life in action and each day I flow with purpose, elegance, and ease.

140

A new cycle is born, with pregnant possibilities on the horizon. Your gift is peace, an aspect of grace and spirit, with your play guided by your heart.

Trust the gift of peace, honoring spirit with your heart and mind in sync.

I courageously use my power with gentleness and strength, opening many doors to bring reconciliation, harmony, and joy.

I share best wishes and blessings, hands of healing light, nurturance for the soul, and constant insightful care.

I weave blessings into the sacred fabric of life. These are the gifts carried across the ancient tides of time.

141

You are going in the right direction and have received a clear sign to initiate focused change. States of grace have been reached through your journeywork, and you claim your personal power.

Follow the soaring joy of your heart's desires, not allowing the illusion of limitation to ground you.

I am the spirit of tenacity.

I am mastering the art of patience in every area of my life.

I am the spirit of patience, with all things possible.

I create only joyful experiences in my loving world.

142

The blue jays sit in silence as the wind holds its breath. The sunset casts a hue of violet lights over the white mystical mountain; directly above a gargantuan cloud hovers, symmetrically rounded like a scoop of whipped-cream in an otherwise clear sky. A mystery unfolds . . .

Establish a determined and focused mindset, and "hit the target" of your desires.

Thinking outside of the box, use your intelligence in different creative ways and try an unconventional angle of action.

Exercise the skills of observation, adaptability, and clowning in clever maneuvers to gain knowledge and share your way of being.

Utilize all of your resources (seen and unseen) in order to accomplish your goals.

All my contracts have been blessed and completed. Freedom and blissful gratitude wash through me.

I now co-create with the higher dimensions, viewing all through the panoramic lens of perfection, to assist the Avatars.

I invite the sacred mystery to reveal itself to me.

143

You are in the Flow. The timing is perfect for the unfolding of the Sun's Golden Radiance of the Heart, by just being where you are—in the here and now.

Set aside ten to fifteen minutes every day to still your thoughts. In quietness, adopt a listening attitude to commune with your inner magic to experience the greatest love of all.

I claim the magic of my life.

I am worthy. I am loveable. I am capable.

144

The Redwood trees, their temples vaulted high, stand mighty in strength and endurance, witnessing the rise and fall of power. These proud monarchs live on, guarding our shores and us, their wayward people.

Humbly honor and give thanks for the Redwood's glorious presence, for God stands before you in these splendid, awe-inspiring trees.

I am strength. I am endurance. I am serenity.

I am thankful for the healing gifts of nature.

145

Stagnation is poison to life. You have the power of choice.

Say "Yes" to living, and keep reinventing yourself anew. Happiness is a choice; so is suffering stagnation.

Refuel with positive emotions by honoring all the challenges and difficulties you encounter. Overcome them—they prepare you and give you resolve—to keep evolving.

I say "Yes to life" and honor all lessons in my life.

I gain strength and confidence as I embrace all of life, contribute, and continue up the escalator of life.

There is nothing that obstructs my I AM Perfection from expressing through my form. "I AM the Light of the World."

146

Following your heart's promptings, and setting clear intentions, puts you into the flow of meeting the right people, in the right circumstances, and with the right results unfolding naturally. The big sabotage trap is when your mind drops into self-judgment and doubt, saying, "What is it I am supposed to be doing?"

Say "Yes" to what your heart affirms. Regulate your feelings, watch your thinking, and remove any judgments, participating, living on purpose, setting intentions, and allowing what materializes to be through acceptance. This is saying "Yes" to embrace your life fully. And Life will respond with a "Yes" to you.

I gratefully accept my highest guidance and illumination while staying flexible and willing to change course if prompted.

I choose to do my very best—doing my very best makes me happy and now I do my best for the sheer pleasure of doing it.

I let go of the inaction of watching TV; it hides the fear of being alive and expressing who I am.

I take action because I enjoy the action. Action is living fully.

I am exactly doing what is most required in the moment.

147

A new consciousness and electronic patterning is birthing with the Earth's evolution. Ether (all-pervading) is the record keeper, the great doorway through time and space. The past records of man show the repetitive patterns of the two diametric poles of opposites competing for superiority. This duality consciousness is coming to a close and being replaced by Oneness—Unconditional Divine Love.

Say goodbye to the misuse of power and greed that supports duality.

I speak my truth from the place of Divine Love and no longer allow my will to be diminished or suppressed if my boundaries are crossed by activity that is not in divine alignment.

I let go of duality thinking which supports separation: who is right and who is wrong, or who is inferior and who is superior.

I release the judgments of duality and embrace the Beingness of Oneness.

I see the pairs of opposites but I am Unity.

148

The key to life is to acknowledge the Greater. When you pour your life into the Greater with your free will, the Greater will then be able to give back perfectly. The active Universal Cycle of giving and receiving brings overwhelming gratitude and humility.

Invest in the Greater through time with spirit each day.

I gratefully receive renewal each day and rest in contentment.

I acknowledge the Greater with every action as my artistry.

149

Evolution, involution, and devolution are cycles of nature. Nature is dynamic and is always changing, never static.

You are part of nature, which is dynamic. The seasons bring change. Allow what no longer supports your highest best, to dissolve into the sea of forgetfulness. You are on a path of transformation.

I am evolving and as I change, I become dynamic.

150

Doubt or fear towards that which is not understood is a human trait. Yet without doubt or fear, there is no incentive to investigate, and there is no learning without investigating. Darkness is a lack of light and fear is a lack of information. Fear becomes false evidence appearing real.

Trust and acknowledge God with all your heart. Then, as you investigate, your path will be directed.

I am free to investigate and find truths that resonate with the wisdom of my soul.

I unlatch my heart to the father of my mind and open my mind to the beauty of the mother in my heart.

I give myself permission to explore a deeper relationship with the ineffable.

I am courageous as I explore and find what is authentic and right for me.

151

Where your attention goes, your energy flows . . .

Your brain is smart; place your attention on your heart.

As my radiant heart glows, creation of kindness and goodwill sows.

Love, wisdom, and power; direction and protection each hour.

Divine will and abundance flows, and all perfection unfolds.

152

Any doubt entertained is a stepchild of fear. All you have to do is show up, be willing, and participate fully.

Follow the tender knowingness of your heart. Be willing. Be open. Listen to your inner promptings and let sunshine radiate through your smile.

I call upon the total accumulation of all my good to come forth into expression through me now.

153

Forgiving yourself is the most important of all actions that you can embrace. When moments of clarity arrive, they can bring deep remorse for what was left unfinished and draw the angels close, creating sacred transformational space. When you can forgive yourself, you can forgive others completely for what was done or not done, moving forward with a fresh canvas for creation to play upon.

Reflect on how the loving angels keep watch over you but cannot intervene or interfere with your free will.

I forgive the flaws and faults of others as I forgive myself. In forgiving, I am released from suffering and become free.

I forgive God—I forgive myself.

I willingly request and accept assistance from my angels in all my endeavors, as I move forward with ease and grace.

154

You teach what your soul desires you to learn. If you don't learn and own the length and breadth of it, you keep teaching it until you own and live it.

You teach what you are required to learn.

I pay close attention to all the lessons presented in my life for my own completion and advancement.

155

Your mind is becoming whole. By allowing inspirational ideas to be held in your mind, they will grow their own desire, which leads to a thinking pattern for manifestation to materialize.

Allow new ideas to come and rest in your mind without talking yourself out of the images.

Divine love is who and what I am, and this is the only presence I express or feel. I align with this truth.

I am manifesting—the will of the Divine—through my mind.

I am manifesting—the love of the Divine—through my heart.

156

True spiritual empowerment is your destiny. Empowerment never abuses or misuses power—through examination, insight comes. Keeping so busy that you don't have to look at your undermining patterns won't work anymore. Transparency and telling yourself the truth lead to humility that creates sacred space and a deep expansion of the heart.

Look at what is not working in your life—all that which you resist.

Accountability is a key to spiritual empowerment as I create new pathways.

I am honest and truthful with myself first and foremost.

157

Following your intuition increases your sensitivity and expands your awareness.

Be true to your own self and listen to your inner promptings.

I have a new role as a director: I AM Divine consciousness, discerning mind, courageous heart, and a conviction of knowingness.

My inner life directs where I am choosing to go with conviction.

I follow what makes my heart sing.

158

Some of the things you are working toward may require adjusting in order for you to move forward, such as letting go of what you have been invested in and building for a long time. You may feel like you are starting all over again. This takes courage. It can feel a lot safer to hold on to the old plans, but if you hold on to the old ways you will find yourself stuck now.

It is a time to be flexible, so rewrite the whole plan for yourself if required. Be willing to step around something or create something new and be courageous. Look for what you are afraid of and find a way to face that fear. Keep finding ways to move on your path. Trust yourself, trust your inner voice, and keep moving.

I am willing to see things in a new way.

I let go of my attachments while keeping a clear vision of my desires and requirements.

159

Light has no concept of right or wrong. Experiences of life are neither good nor bad; only thinking makes them so through judgment. There is no good or evil in the higher octave of light, only Perfection.

Be kind and forgiving to yourself; everything in your life has a higher purpose.

I choose to be at peace with myself.

I am Light.

160

Grace is a willingness to be grateful and to express gratitude. Gratitude takes you out of selfishness, and draws generosity and bounty to you. Just as you require food to nourish your body, you require gratitude to replenish your coffers. The giving of gratitude opens an abundance of doors and invites a beauty with an intricate expansion.

In gratitude, find a heartfelt way to daily acknowledge the small and large blessings in your life. Increase your desire to be grateful.

I fill my coffers with light-hearted play, joy, and gratitude each day.

I walk through open doors to the greater abundance carried by the momentum of gratitude.

161

A bridge of light surrounds you; as you accept more of your higher mental body and electronic patterning into your being, there is a joining of forces, making you invincible. As the mind of God conceives and the heart of God manifests, refinement results.

Do not let the mischief of the altered ego intervene. The ego would have you evaluate your performance from the past and limit you.

I say "No" to self-judgmental thoughts when they arise.

I say "Yes" to joyous new ideas circulating freely within me.

Now is the time to evaluate from the future.

162

Lots of disappointment equals lack of discipline. All the disappointments experienced get stuffed down and stored in the shadow recesses in your body.

As disappointments resurface in your awareness, simply lovingly accept them as they wash through you and release.

My discipline realigns with my Higher Self, and freedom alights.

I now welcome constructive discipline in my thoughts. I am in charge of my thinking. Each thought is a prayer. I choose to be mindful of what I am praying in each moment.

It is OK for the mind to idle in silence, as emotions come up to be released—without trying to process or label them.

163

"Would you really investigate insanity?" Duality, discord, and imperfection will not be supported in your future.

Walk through each limitation, and experience freedom by trusting in your own powers of discrimination. Give yourself permission to participate and experience something prejudged as having no value. The outcome may be a delightful surprise, and things are never the way they appear.

Oh Lord of Life, I require to become free from my limiting human desires and to be filled with Divine Desires now!

I choose to walk away from drama and discord.

I am free. I use my time wisely. I am perfection unfolding.

164

The flame of purification is an invincible shield against the sinister forces of negative thoughts and feelings that are currently held within the mass consciousness. The flame guides me to see and act with affection, kindness, and benevolence.

Invite the flame of purification to flow through you, extending 19 feet out and encircling you.

I am no longer guided by resentment or feeling angered by the old limited views of wanting things a certain way.

I radiate peace and good will.

I am invincible and peaceful in outer confusion and chaos.

165

Children hold no judgments.

Be childlike, letting go of all hardened beliefs. Any judgments held get saddled into your emotional body. Let them go! Cultivate instead childlike qualities of curiosity, play, lots of laughter, living in the moment, abandoning worries, imagination, creativity, and pure joy.

I am a miracle and every moment I have is a gift. What will I do with that gift?

I am laughter, I am curious, and I am light-hearted.

166

What you feel, you make real. You cannot manifest with your mind if your emotions (your feeling body) do not agree.

Write down in a journal what you are willing to accept. In the back of the journal write down what you no longer accept.

I no longer accept discord in the thoughts I entertain.

I AM an unlimited Being.

I AM an Untouchable.

167

What is it that you desire, what is it that you require, and what is it that you aspire to in life?

Give yourself the time to fertilize your heart, mind, body, and spirit. Each day spend time quietly with yourself. Go for a walk in nature or take ten minutes and do something inspiring for you. Early in the morning or late at night—you know your own rhythm.

I create a beautiful life aligned with my soul's higher calling while nourishing the whole of me.

I replenish my body, mind, and spirit each day, while living my purpose.

168

Children create through joy and their imagination endless stories, always moving on to their next creation. Within duality, adults create stories, believe them, and in so doing perpetuate them in their outer reality over and over again. Experiences of life are neither good nor bad. In letting go of judgment, criticism, and blame you set yourself free.

Stand guard over your senses. Learn to look upon things without allowing their discord into your feeling world. Choose to change your inner story, letting go of judgment and blame. Playing the act of victim will no longer work. You are free to choose how you see your circumstances.

My thoughts create my world. I am free to co-create from my inner vibrant life, which navigates my outer life experiences.

169

Judgment leaves a residue in your feeling body called emotions through the wrong use of your will. You now are capable of knowing right action without it being called right or wrong.

Experience life simply by allowing yourself to follow what is resonating for you from your heart . . . what is saying "Yes" to you . . . what is calling to you on the path of Mastery.

I choose to replace judgment with Resonance.

I follow what resonates with me on my path of Mastery.

170

Every act committed in the absence of Love is really an act of insanity. Behind all insanity is fear acting itself out.

Weekly forgive everyone, including yourself, and keep your emotional body crystal-clear.

My sense of self-worth is not dependent on the opinions of others.

I forgive all who have crossed my path and I recognize that they did not really know what they were doing.

Every act of fear is a call for help. I invite the light of Love to assist.

171

The human self always has an agenda. The Christ Self has no agenda except perfection.

For every single person that you interact with, even the most challenging and hurtful, remember this: "They were always doing their best."

I, in the midst of me, can do all things.

172

The life force that beats your heart, which sustains life in your body, is perfect. Your free will colors and re-qualifies that perfection with whatever beliefs or emotions you are embracing.

Monitor and take charge of your thoughts, and let go of old beliefs. Develop the art of resting in your heart, your inner perfection. From this place, your authentic expression unfolds with your unique flavor of who you truly are.

My goal is zero conflict while being absolute peace and absolute harmony. This state draws me into the sacred heart of God.

I place my awareness within the contentment of the heart as I interact in my environment.

I am the life force and I invite my inner perfection to shine through.

173

Resistance to Love has created all the lessons you have experienced.

Earnestly listen to the wisdom of the Inner Presence, which places you perfectly where you are required. Life then cooperates, and guides you toward the greatest possible service and advancement.

With purity and transparency of heart, I walk the path before me.

I let my Light shine with luminosity as I surrender to the longing of my soul.

I am worthy. I am lovable.

174

When you give purpose to your life, it is incredible what you can create and accomplish.

Say "Yes" to life and make your own personal and constructive choices for life; this begins your personal path towards greater freedom.

I have freedom to choose, and I choose to create and accomplish that which is most meaningful according to my life's purpose.

I can do and achieve anything I place my attention upon. I take one small step at a time.

I choose health and wealth for my body, mind, and spirit.

I am capable. I am smart enough. I am supported and protected.

175

Choose to live from the inside out, and life will unveil the mysteries and perfection of the Universe. It is a path of ease, effortlessness, and grace by choosing peace, divine love, and life!

Expect the Universe to continually reveal to you more of life's mysteries and perfection.

I am responsible for how I feel, and I choose to feel joy, peace, and divine love in each moment.

176

Divine Love is the only Law.

Do your very best in anything you do.

I choose to feel love; I choose to radiate love.

177

Rebirth is occurring; you are coming out of darkness that now opens a new vision. Any changes occurring will be for the best. They bring a fresh outlook with an elegant perspective. Creativity and ideas will flow anew and you will see the truth in things you could not see before. Even what you considered wasted time will ultimately work to your benefit.

Continue going with the flow and follow your heart with the highest outcome manifesting for you.

Everything in my life is of value, even the pruning. As I evolve, I manifest my highest divine potential.

I welcome the ever-new dawning of fresh vision and creativity as I embrace change and follow my heart.

178

Spirituality is about your saying "Yes" to life, realizing and living your passion, and giving yourself permission to fulfill your dreams. It is about understanding the nature of yourself, your world, and how that relates to Source.

Express yourself fully. Stop seeking permission from anyone else to fulfill your true heart's desire. You are never given a dream, wish, or hope without an opportunity to make them into reality. What is it you are willing to contribute to the call of your life?

I give myself permission to passionately fulfill my dreams and my purpose for living at this time period.

179

It is time to come forth into your position of leadership. You are an important part of the key.

You are a leader in how you live your life and how you choose to show up in the world around you. As a conscious leader, you lead from your inner compass aligned with integrity, compassion, and your miraculous oneness. This inner compass allows you to navigate power successfully in the outer world in a way that is unique to you. You—are the ultimate Leader.

I am awed by the synchronicities, the gift of the universe, to bring an accelerated awareness of my place of service.

I am a leader guided by my inner guidance, the driver that directs where I choose to go or how I show up in life.

180

May the Divine Flame consume forever all past and present mistakes, their cause and effect, and all undesirable creations for which the personality is responsible.

Invoke the Divine Law and Divine Justice now, to adjust the outer activity of trickery to be revealed and reconciled.

I am clarity, calm, and practical when disclosing a trickery. I share my observation with no defense necessary and release.

I am not responsible for the lessons that individuals are learning, who have wronged me or caused disturbance.

I engage in activities that lead me towards inspiration (an upward spiral) and move away from what feels flat or burdensome (a downward spiral).

I am guided by the moment-to-moment impulse of "The Eureka Moment" in all my choices of engagement.

181

You can only see <u>one</u> angle and unknown are the forces at play or the condition that created a scenario for an individual.

Resentment is a milder form of hate when held against persons that you hold in judgment. Thoughts and feelings are the creative power. Set your intent to release resentment.

I am the perfect creative thought and feeling present in my mind and heart.

182

Each night, before going to sleep, consciously send Love to everyone whom has harmed you in any way. In time this will all heal.

Return cupid's arrow to create a deeper state of divine love within.

I am resting in the softness of my own heart and sending gentle rays of benediction.

183

Divine intelligence and presence is the only force active in your life.

Know that there is nothing hidden that cannot be revealed to you.

I compel every thing I need to know, to be revealed to me instantly.

I am guided moment to moment; I trust in the highest outcome to manifest for myself and others.

184

You cannot expand as long as you have an emotional opinion about anyone else. It is stifling to your progress.

Monitor your opinions and beliefs.

I am the Perfect Harmony of my thoughts, feelings, and actions.

185

The phrase "that was intense" implies tension. There is no tension in what you do, only ease and joy.

No longer strain after anything.

I am calm and certain in attitude, resting in the ease of Beingness.

I am joyful and relaxed.

186

Know that in all things you are guided.

Seek out knowledge and full details; in divine timing you will know what direction to go. Demand to know and see clearly. In moments when the mind becomes befuddled bring your awareness back to knowingness.

I trust in my inner knowingness to reveal the plan that I am to follow.

187

Harmony draws all good things to you.

Invite the divinity within to flow into everything in your life, which washes and sparkles all into perfection.

God dwells within me as my Divine Inner Presence—come forth, govern and solve situations harmoniously and immediately.

188

The Universal energy that flows through me is naturally harmonious.

What you resist persists. Pay attention to what you are resisting, which is experienced as discontentment or unhappiness. When you embrace what is—it dissolves.

I embrace everything in my life and shrink from nothing.

My life flows harmoniously.

189

Know that nothing inharmonious can touch your inner beingness, which is invincible and protected.

Monitor the old habit of dwelling upon conditions that disturb the mind and stir up the emotions for it gives your power away.

I repel any destructive elements from my being and world.

I now create empowering experiences in my loving world.

190

Dwelling on an imperfection in another becomes a quality pushed into ones own experiences.

Be not concerned with the outer personality of discordant individuals. Instead affirm and dwell on the divinity that lies within them.

I verbally clear imperfect observations by saying: "Cancel . . . Cancel . . . Cancel. I am divine; you are divine."

I salute the divinity in you.

191

When the heart/body are open to feeling gratitude for the gifts received, the universe is able to shower more treasures and bounty!

Invite the One Almighty Intelligence, Power, Light, and Self-Sustained element of abundance to bless your life.

I am receiving and accepting financial acknowledgement, with joyful light-heartedness, for my creative endeavors.

Open the floodgates of abundance, now, in every area of my life.

192

Human sympathy qualifies the feelings that are focused on imperfection and intensifies the imperfection already manifesting. Divine compassion holds the attention, anchored in Great Spirit—producing perfection.

Disengage from listening to repeated patterns of despair, which is a chosen downward spiral. Despair is a narcotic, which soothes the mind into indifference and dissipates the listener's vitality. Focus on the person's highest light and release.

I am drawn to beauty and inspirational surroundings.

I empower perfection through Divine Compassion.

193

Creative block is just a fallow period. It is a period of time for the subconscious mind to take a breather, readying itself to take a different approach.

Join a group or class that supports you in producing in a structured environment. Take a trip somewhere you've never considered or try something totally new that appears interesting to you. Play the "what if" game, being wild in your considerations. Do something that feeds your inner spirit and that nourishes the whole of you.

I am a unique willing expression of God.

I release the fears of failure, the misguided companion of humiliation and rejection.

I am loving what I do, doing it for the love/joy in the moment of creation and release . . . I am not responsible for the consequences.

I am risking, surviving exposure, which breeds self-confidence and freedom—to thrive!

194

The mulberry leaf becomes a silk robe through patience.

Adapt the pace of nature: her secret is patience. Everything that slows us down, forces patience, or that sets us back into the slow cycles of nature, is beneficial. Pruning becomes an instrument of grace.

From Beingness, I manifest and express my full healing potential, gifts, and talents. I surrender my life to the pruning process to reveal its authentic beauty.

I am trusting and patient with divine timing and plan for my life, to manifest in its perfection.

195

The giant sequoia tree sleeps within its tiny seed, and the durable oak tree sleeps within the acorn. The bird waits within the egg, and God waits for recognition within us to emerge.

We the people are awaking . . .

I AM the navigator.

Made in the USA
Charleston, SC
29 June 2012